A light mazed

A Light Mazed

Collected Poems with illustrations

by Stephen Kirin

The Kirins

Published by

KIRIN Press

Bury St Edmunds

Suffolk

UK

www.stephenkirin.com

Editing by Lorna Kirin

Printed in the UK

First Edition 2023

ISBN 978-1-909769-32-8

For Lorna

Poems

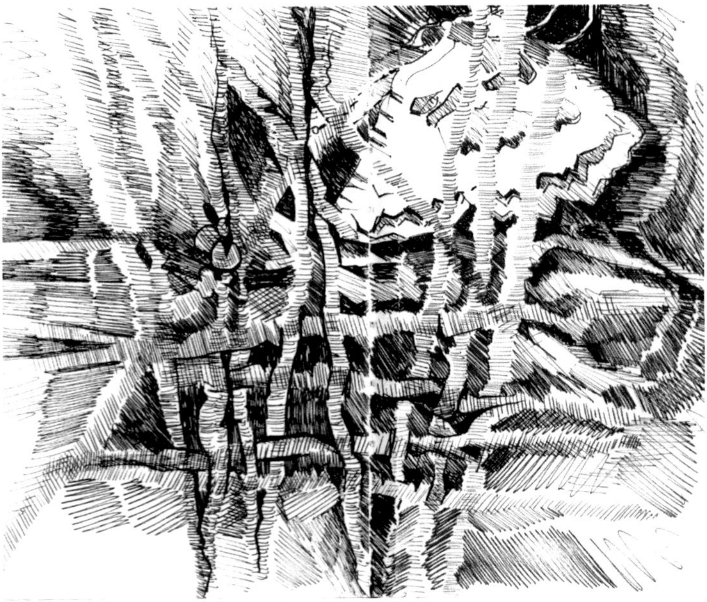

The Light Maze

You're born you die

And the rest is all at once

The light wave

Pools round events

The craze the laze

There is only one day

Inbetween dreams

To get nothing done

Old young young old

A band of gold

Sat on the horizon

And buttered the land

Sunset on someone's rhyme

Coloured in time.

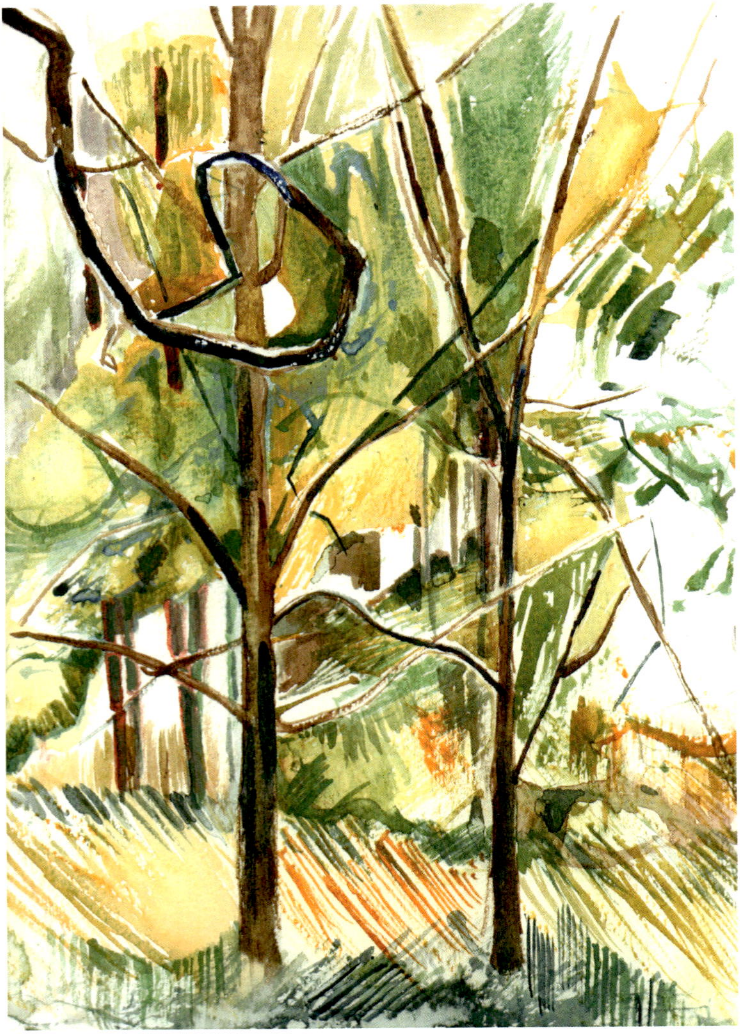

March

When plum blossom and snowdrops meet
And March snow goes nowhere
I bury my face deep in your hair
Because of Spring
Because of warming
Because of drinking in the sap
I lie in the lap of the year
A bluebell spear and a thunderclap
The ducks flew and down fluttered
The white of my eye
Between the thaw
No season for why.

The Siskin

Is it easy to be a bird?
Flying through forests undisturbed
As easy as being human
Making castles in the sky
Squawking why to broken eggs
Fixing smiles to alphabets
And all without wings
The birds watch us sing
Our songs of sixpence
To the siskin
And in truth we're just colours
To each other
That don't know if they'd swap
For one another.

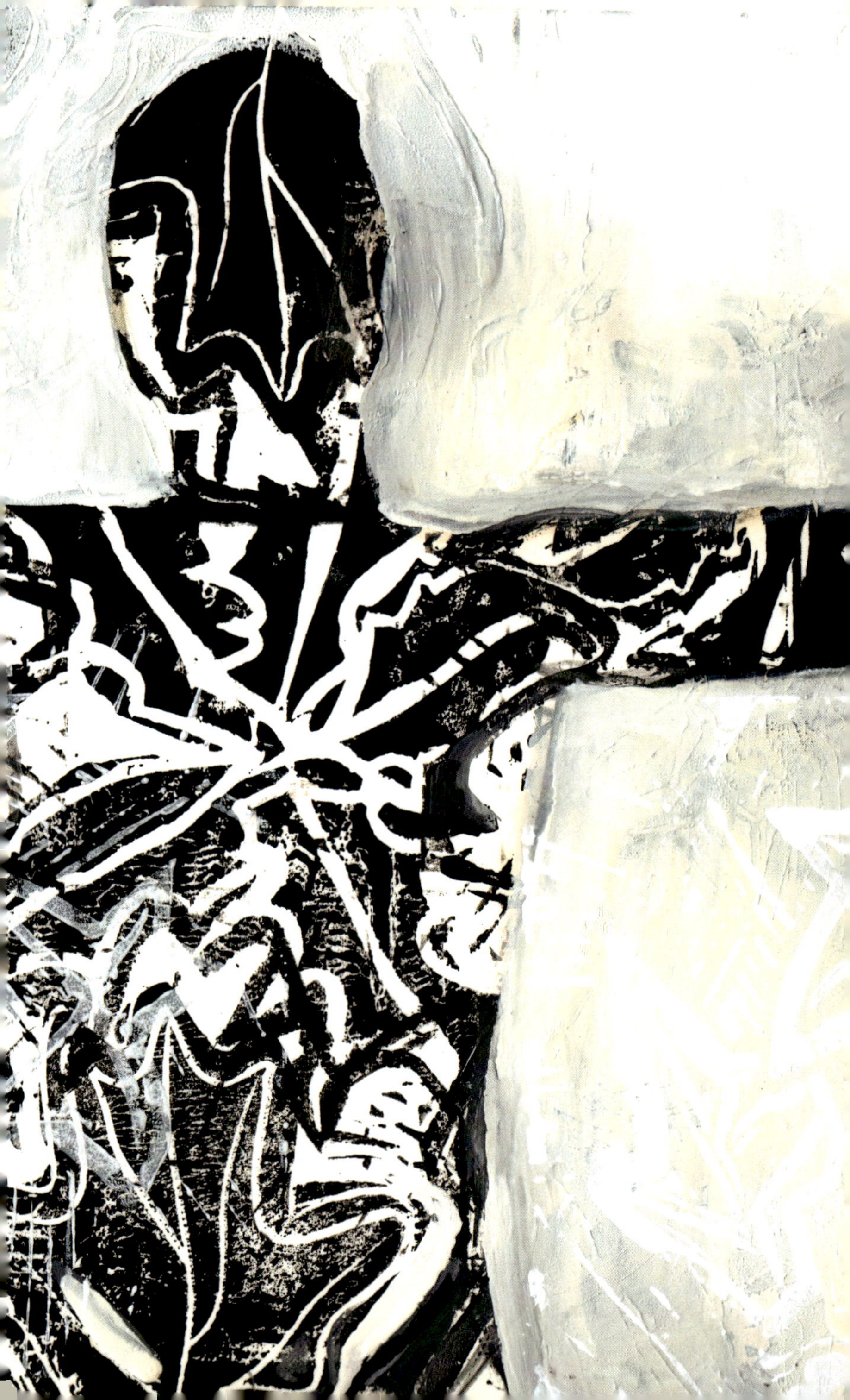

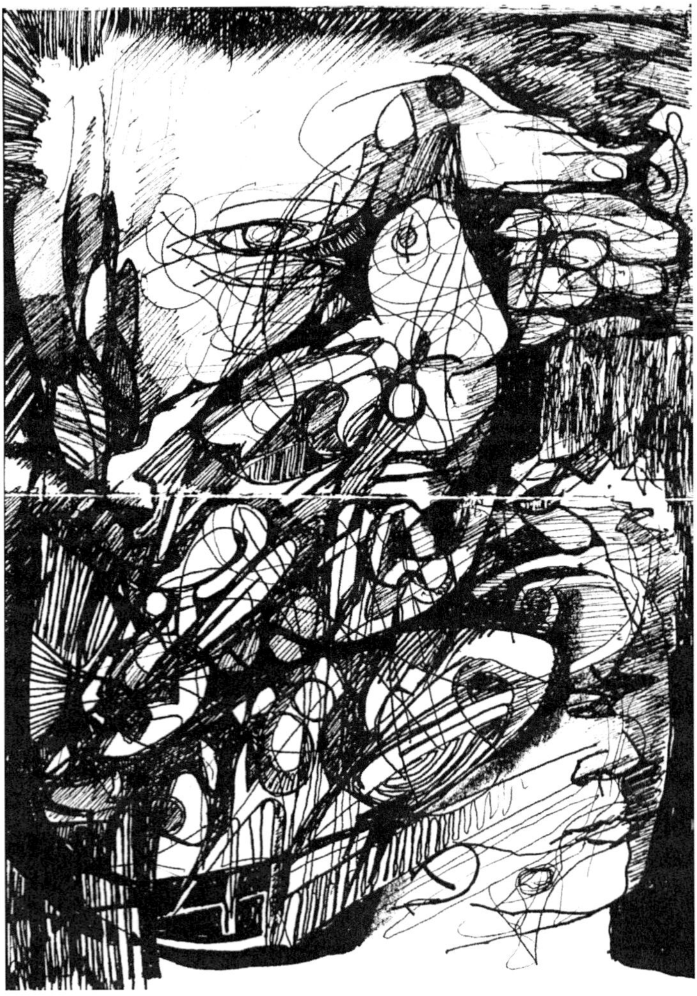

Our job

Our job is to make hay
While you can
Fill the clouds with rain
Before the drain
Butter up the sun
Before becoming toast
Our job is to dream the day real
With senses that feel
The nonsense of being sentient
But not seeing.

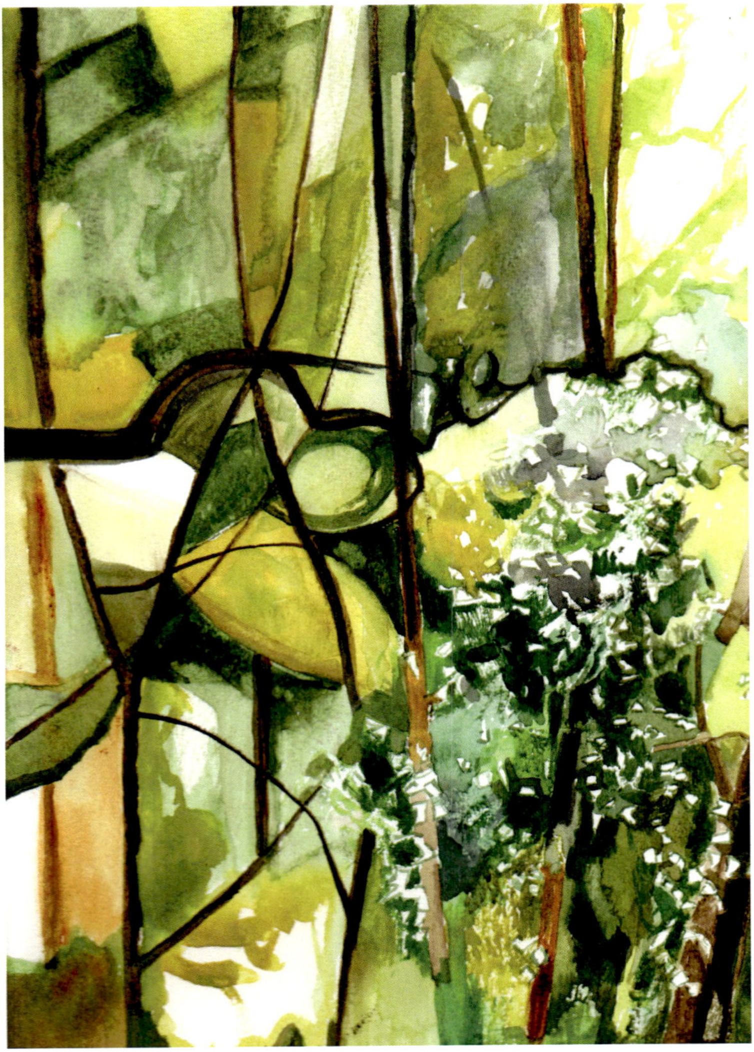

Trinity

Eating morels and cracking walnut shells
From the trees and of the wood
Another brain clenched it's fissures
Grasped the rod and held the beam
Of the pulverising machine
Eat the brain to gain the wisdom
Brain of wood and of tree
Brain of man a trinity
Stories are spores that float from shells
Reworked and unconsumed
Then reimagined as skull of air
Not really there.

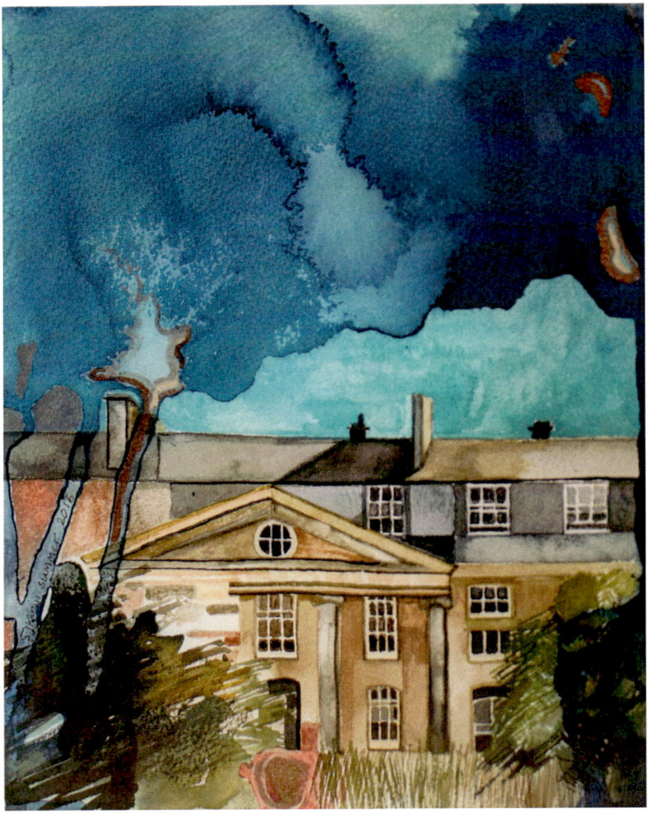

Blue

The middle exhale

Is blue of sky and ocean

Kingfisher flash horizontal

Fuchsia beetle metallic and vertical

Jumps into the blues

The point where topaz meets

The trajectory of my blue eye

And ocean calms the commotion

In one breath.

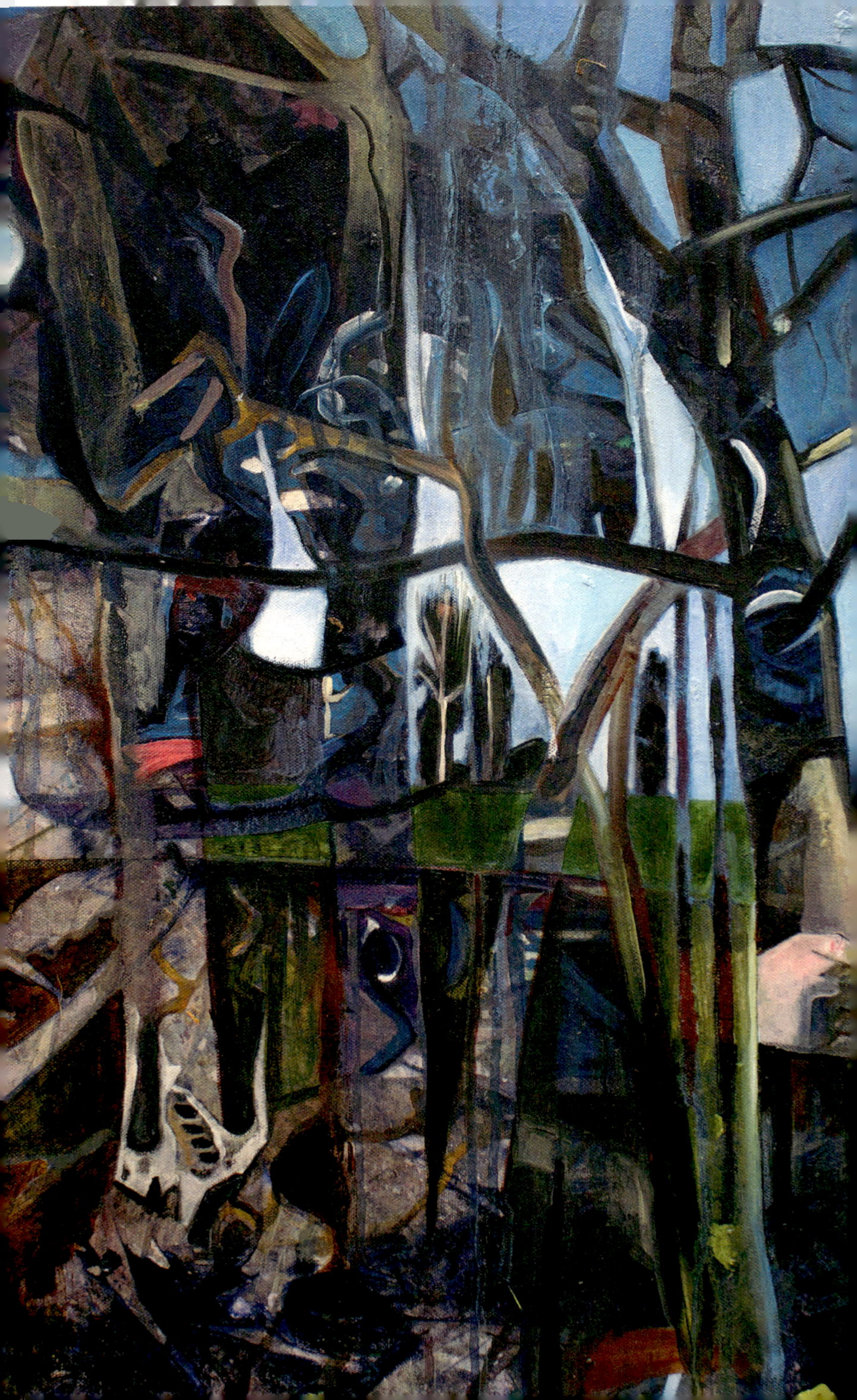

Vernal Equinox

I felt like Iamus

Planting violets amidst bugloss

Cushioned by vipers honeyed light

Fed and safe ground down if there was a bite

This was March under trees and bees

Layer upon layer unfurling

Vying for advantage

Buying an hour in sunshine

The difference between frog spawn

And the heron's bill.

Arm span to height day to night

Same size feet as a tree's shoe

Making tracks like the mushrooms do.

This was a storm in a muntjac skull

By and large.

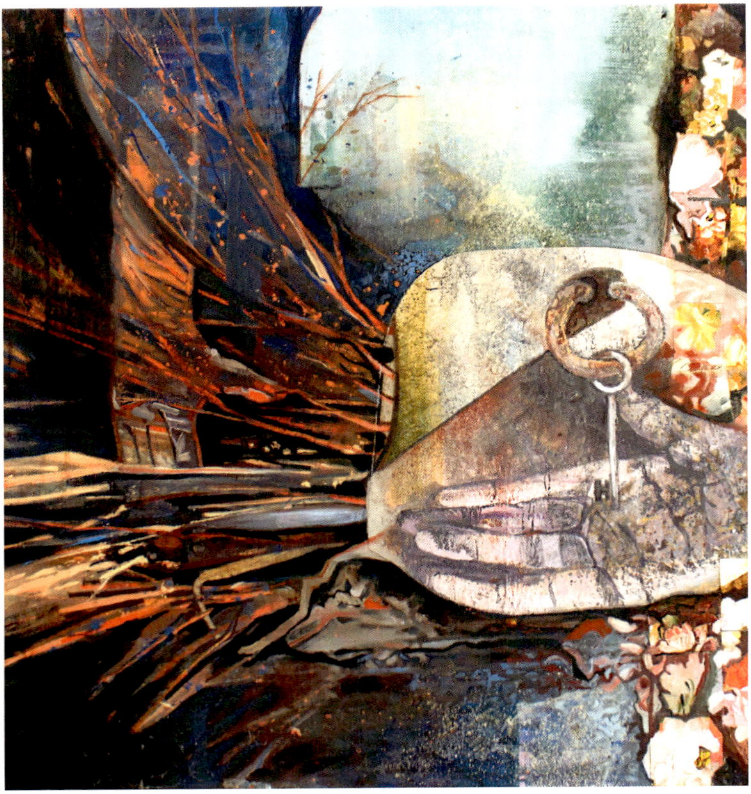

Walpurgisnacht

On the banks of the cursed buttercup
Bittersweet gulped amiss
A misty sweep
Of a Brocken spectre
Kissed toad
Floated up from murk below
My shadow an algae
And sodden vapour slept on moss
An ague doss
Or a broken dream
Any which way
I won't chance a witch's lap
On Walpurgisnacht.

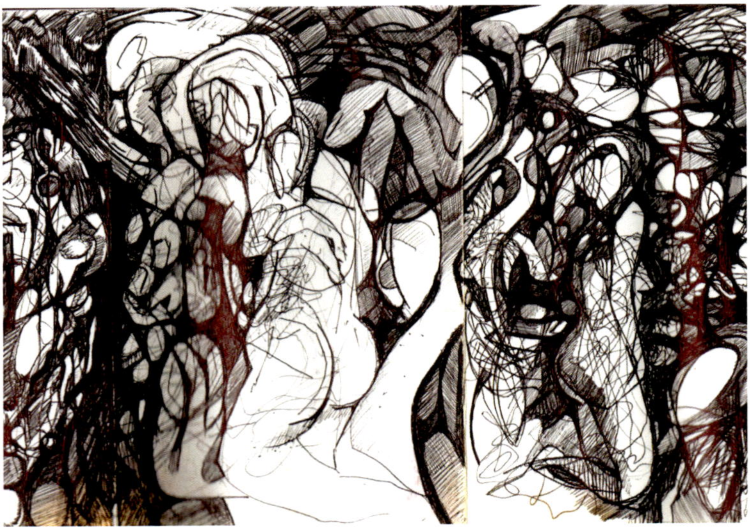

Copley Hill

Copley Hill is in the middle

Of birth and death

Only a hill because the rest isn't

Only a message because of what's adjacent

Addenbury and Wandlebrookes

The barrows of death's past

Via Devana at half mast

Copley Hill divides the two

Borrows time to fuel the view

Agog Magog to the last.

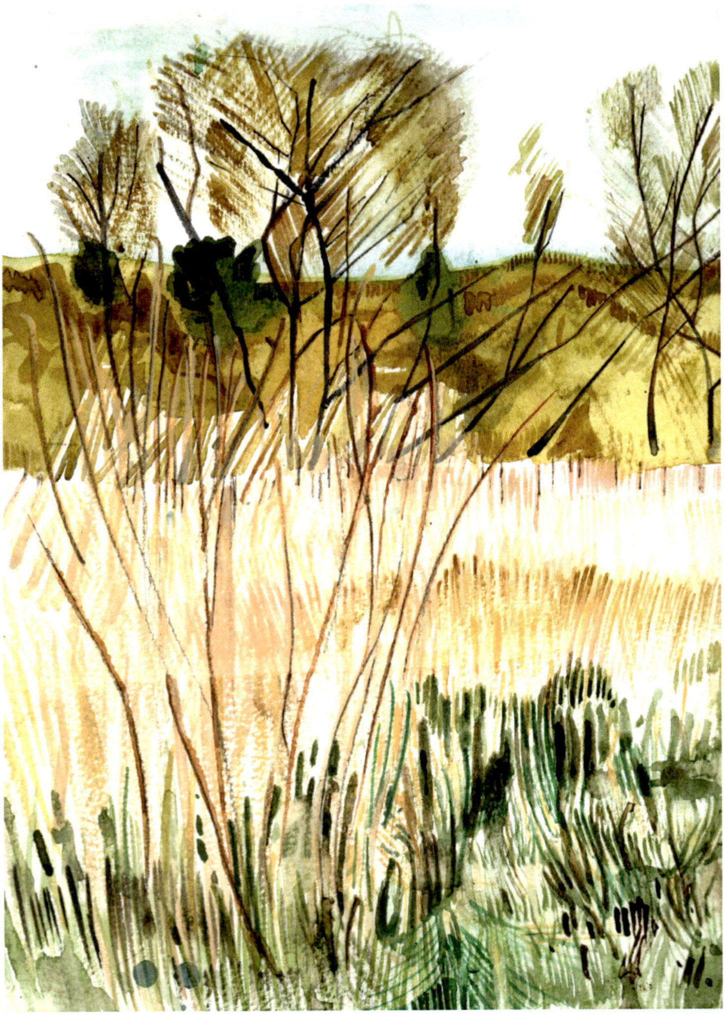

Lammas Meadow

I walked in a floodplain yesterday
A bleached white Lammas meadow
Swaying grass a reed in a hollow vessel
Piping the lines between earth and sky
As the Lark drifts by.
Trying to respond with my palette
With pale on white and mist at night
Drying paint in a stark nearly not landscape
The long tailed tits wave like flits
Written to forebears and future
And the floodplain swells
Like a tear ducts prism
The next day's mist
Hung written like a trace of paper
For my daughter over Lark's sing of bright water
Hand in hand with the ring on her finger
Walking the lines of the land.

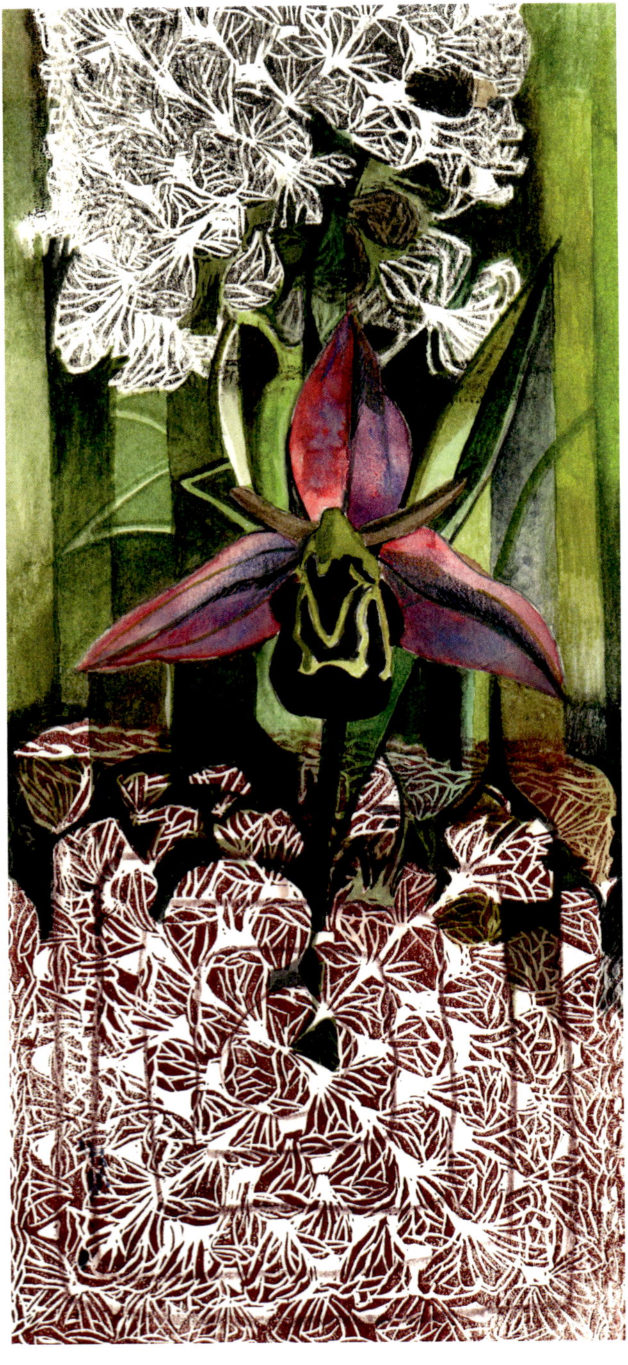

The Carpenter Bee

The carpenter bee made a hole in the willow

Salix to hexagon the tree may go

They'll suffer another

After the woodpecker comes

And I'll watch it change

From the cradle to its graven image

Nesting on this ball of dirt

That fed us for a while

Before dissembling it's atoms

Like Democritus said.

A wink of the eye splits the aspirin

That was my pillow

And we'll spiral again around the hand that feeds

This form of us

This swarm of dust.

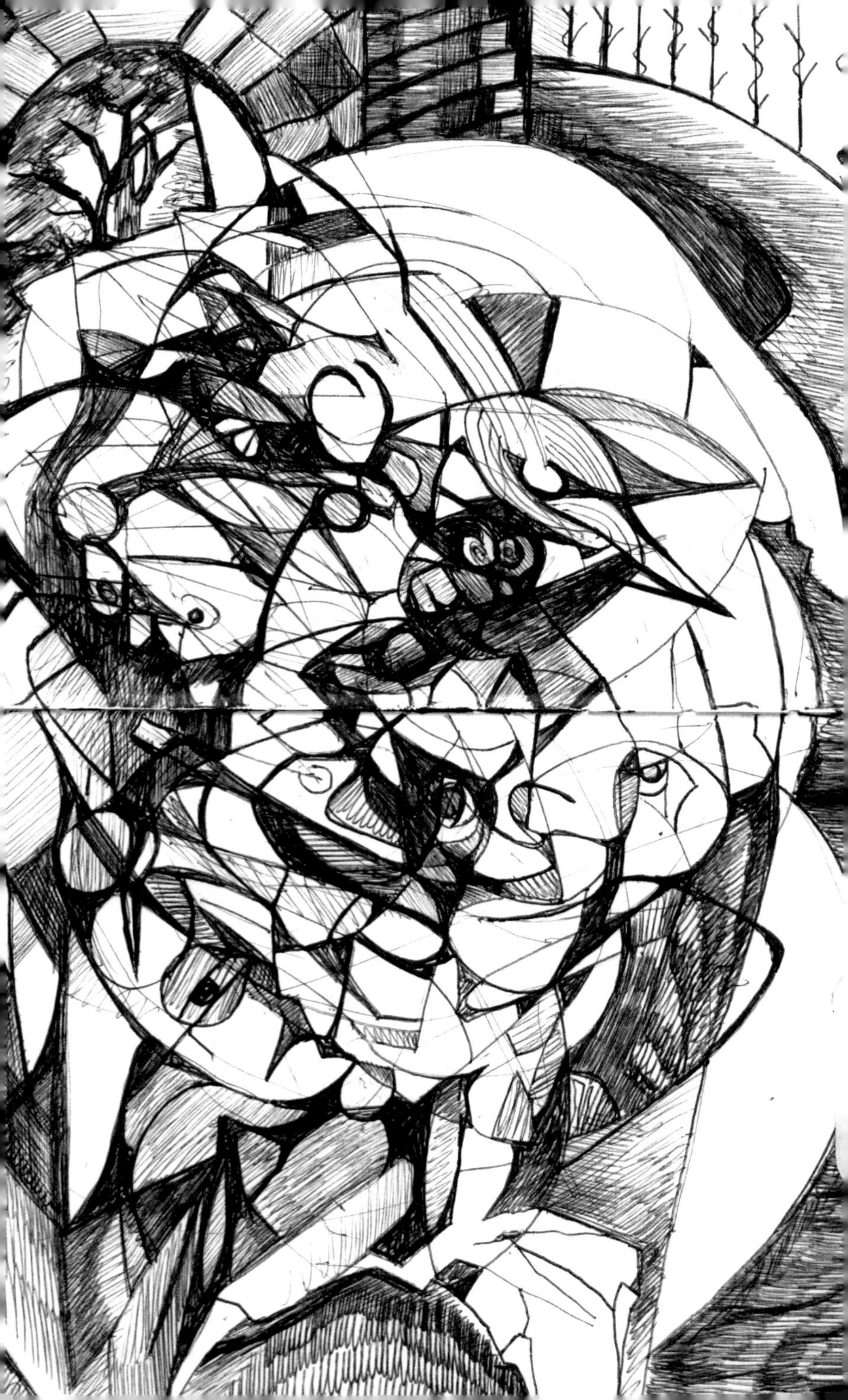

The Longest Day

The longest day
Is as long as the trail
Of my finger on her skin
Then someone else's dog
Killed the fledged blackbird.

After interruption all involved
Looked at me for a moment
Red blood fell with the rising sun
Summer with lips and poppies
As long as the day was red
Traced by my finger had begun.

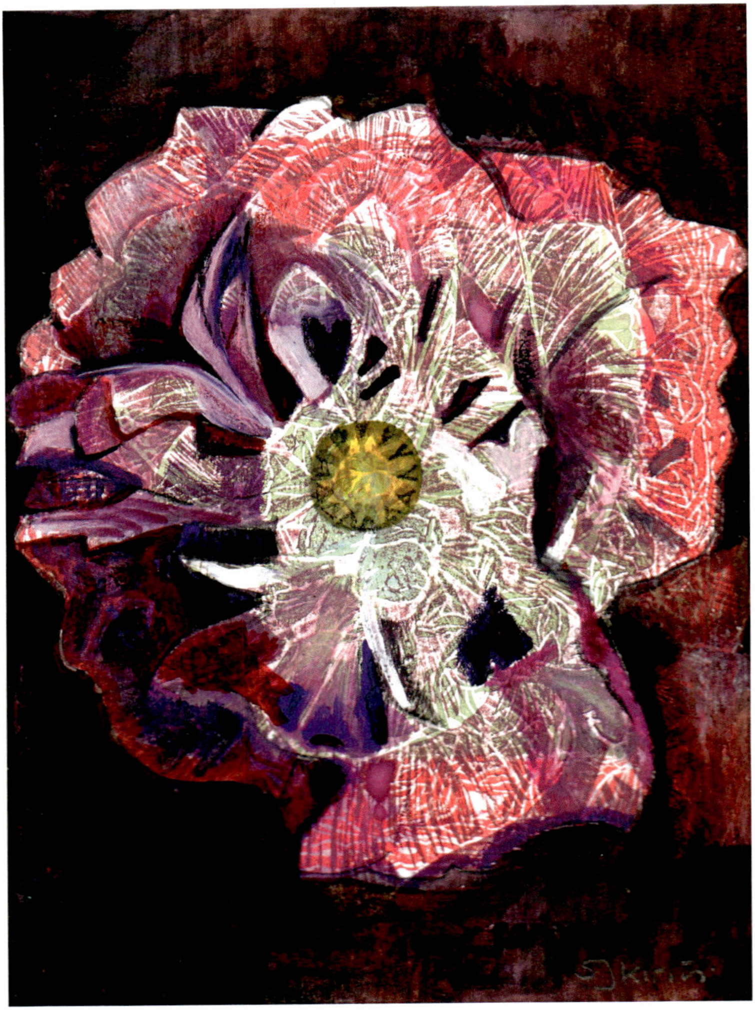

Sol

The howling net
Of summer sun
Febrile fecund irresistible
Poppy smothered
Senses bookended
Between withered dark
Cells buzzing release
Of a shrouded forget
In forest green
All on wing
The iris blue
Looks for you
Casting no shadow
Ophrys apifera
Is wearing weather
And nearer nearer
A sun seen scent
Draws us together.

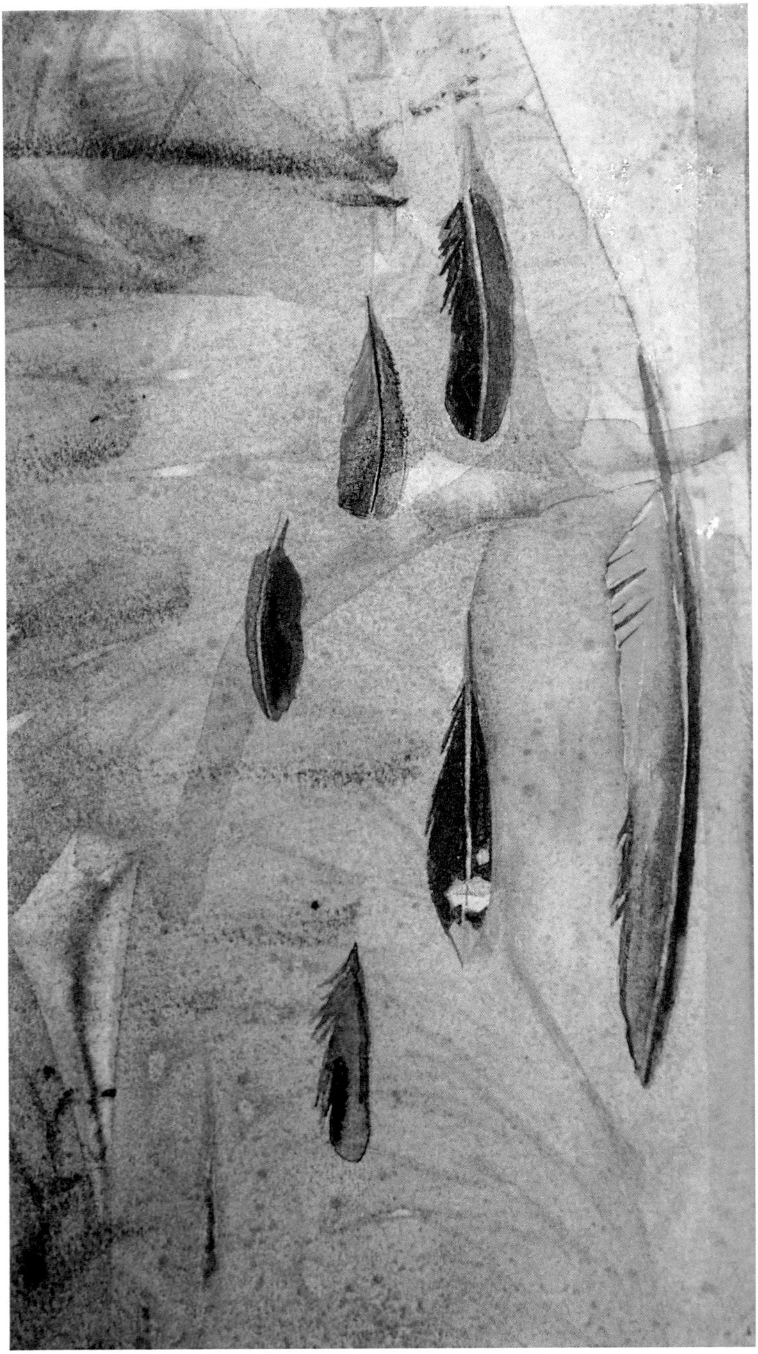

The Drop

A jug of ale in the countryside

Fair end to a day

Stacking hay

Then dropped and no more

Four sherds of mottled ware

Three hundred years later

Reformed a little

But won't hold time

Or wrestle successfully

With memories arm

Except I glimpsed him

Standing there

Because a drop is the same

Everywhere.

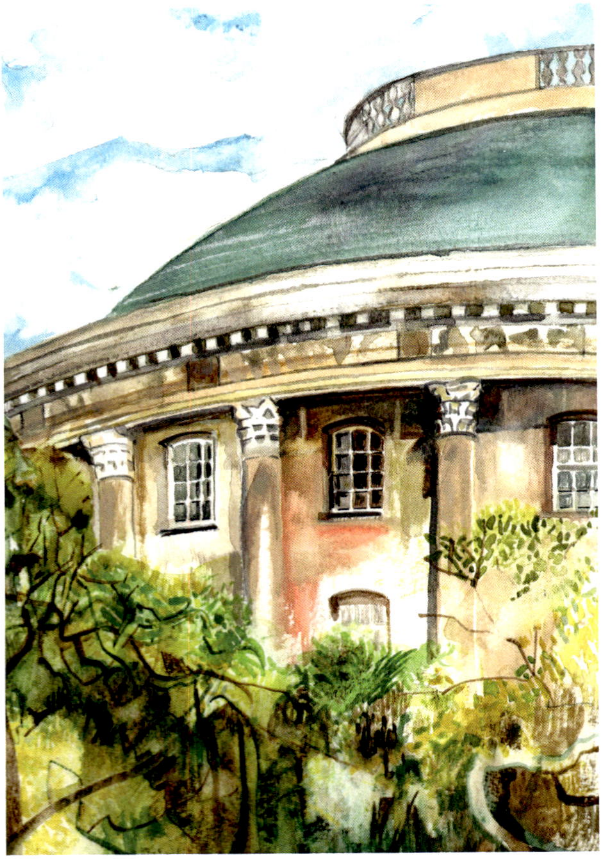

The 19th

An interstice
Of sunny weather
Spotlights the nineteenth
A day remaindered
For parents' funerals
And their forevers
Shared that day
With the head of state
And all I can do is correlate
The arcs of time
That slice and rhyme
Space incarnate
Sewing the sides
Of their interstice.

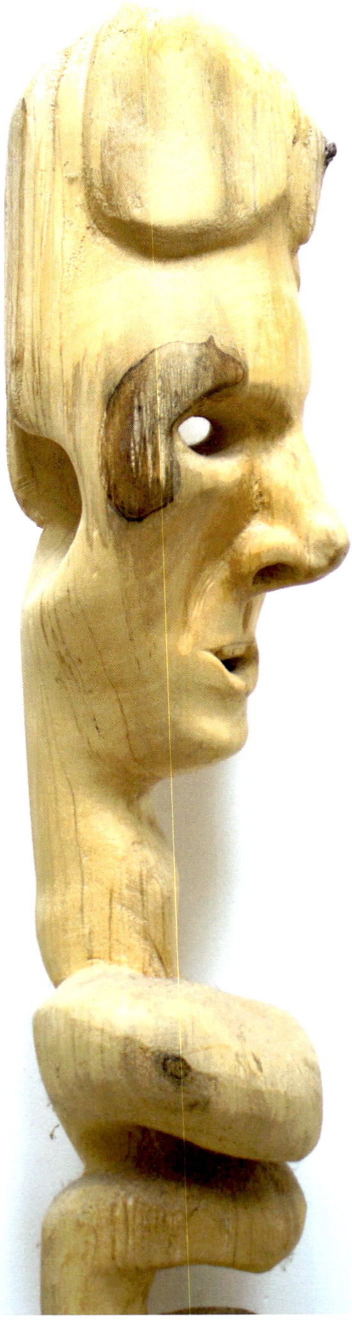

Longshore

If longshore drift played with my face
My nose would be in a different place
But instead it's just a contact
A retina in a lighthouse
Contracts between skin and bone
Lighting spits of memory
Bits of you and bits of me
Drifting aimlessly.

Feathers

It's as if all the birds
In every weather
Had dropped every feather
The weight sometimes
Of all those whys
A ton of lead
Or a ton of words unsaid
Down on a feathered bed
The weight belies
The width of squawks
When the birds are dead
And they sing remembering
When a ton of song
Weighed the same as
Fly away Autumns'
Flu away fall
Feather or not
Bird at all.

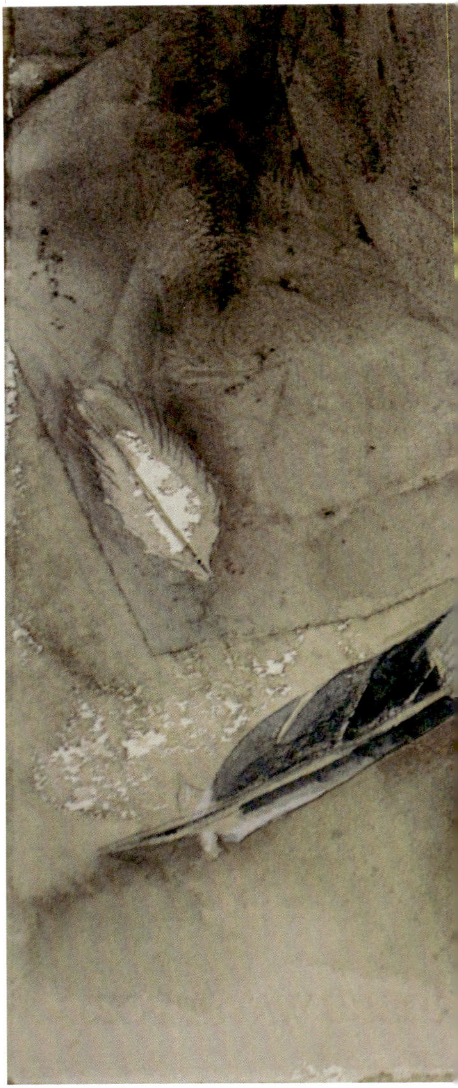

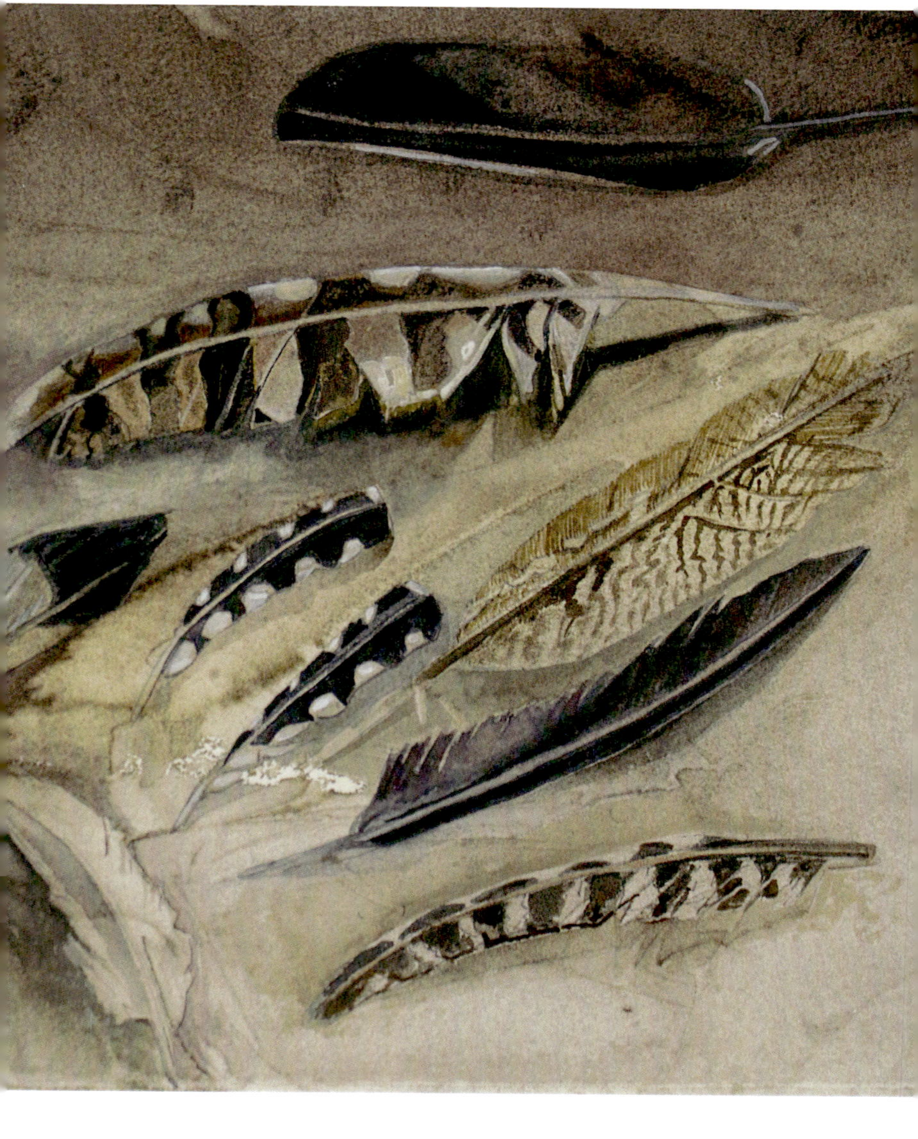

You Fall Like She Leaves

You fall like she leaves
An Autumn coloured harvest moon
And red of fox across baked bare earth.
You fall like shadows cross
Lit up dreams of sated heavy green.
The first smell of earth cooling
Is fevers broken leaves
And dancing madder clouds
A North South mound of earth
Traversed East West by Oak balanced
On silence coming.

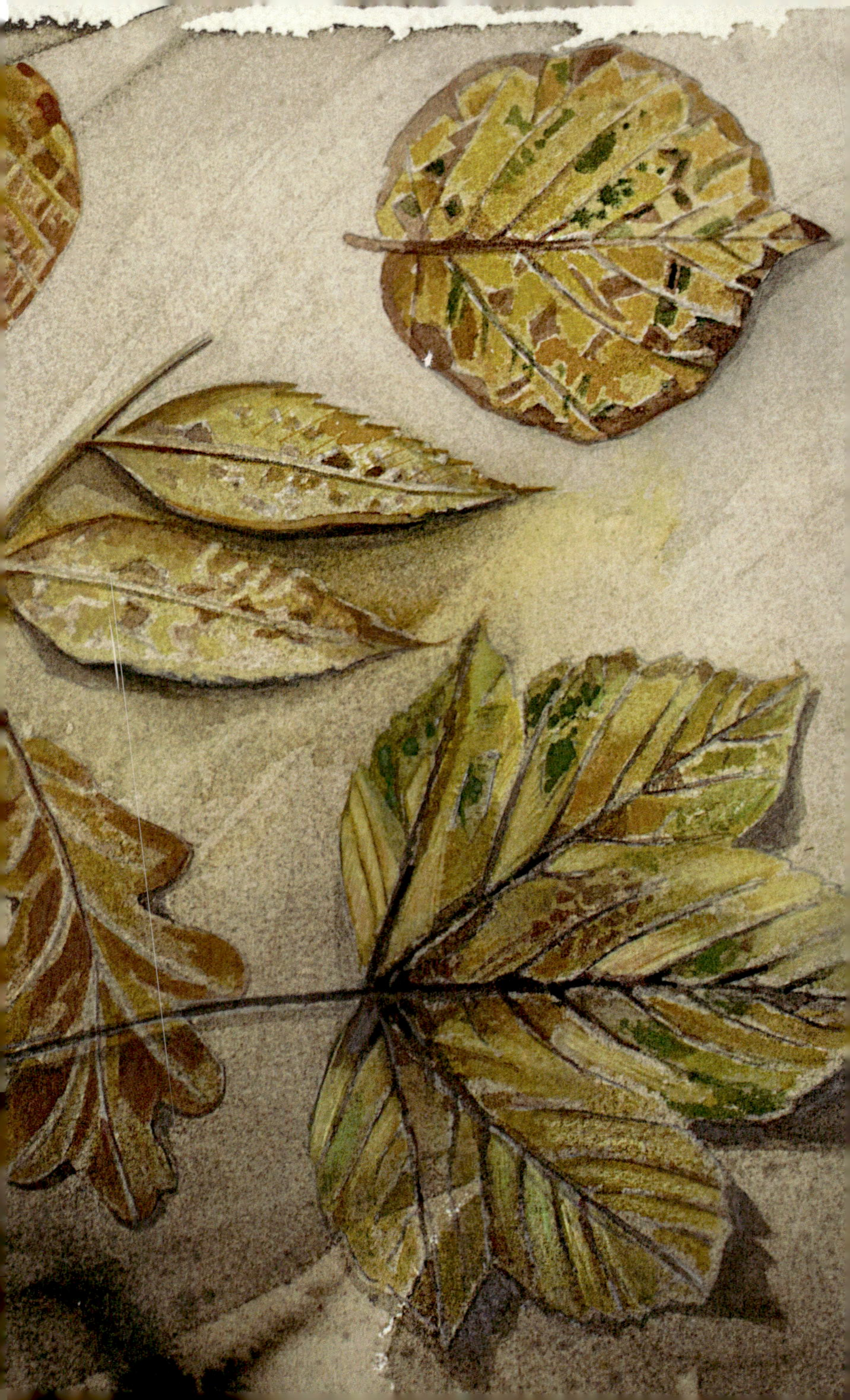

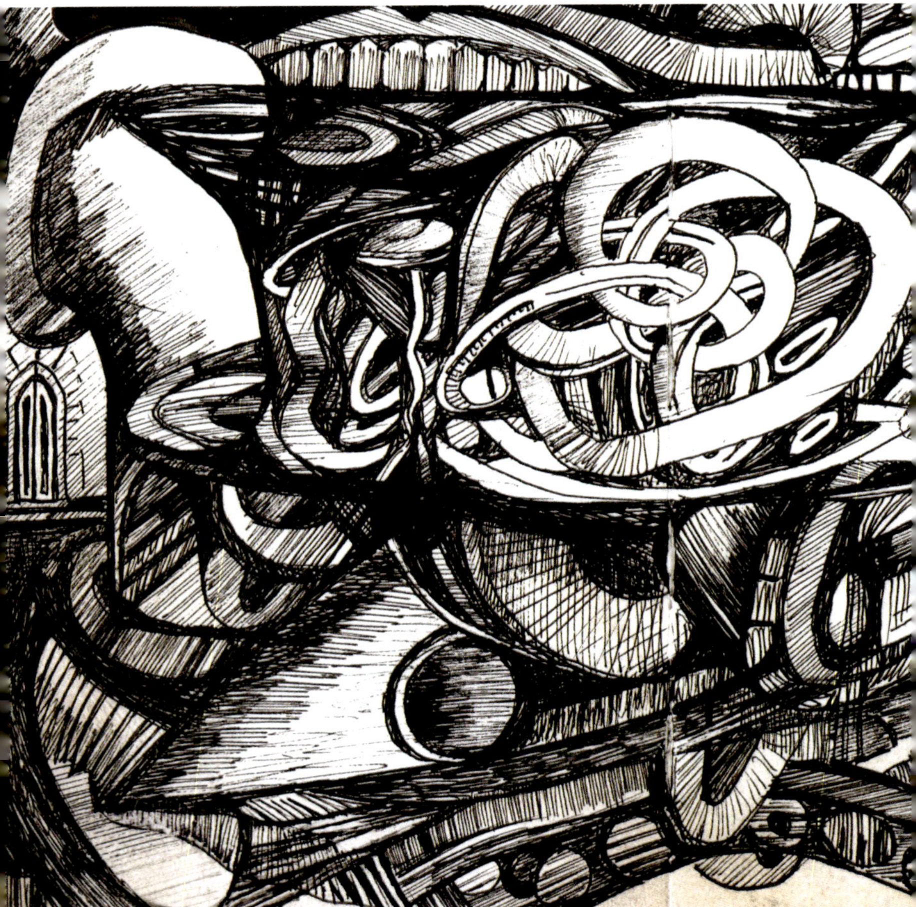

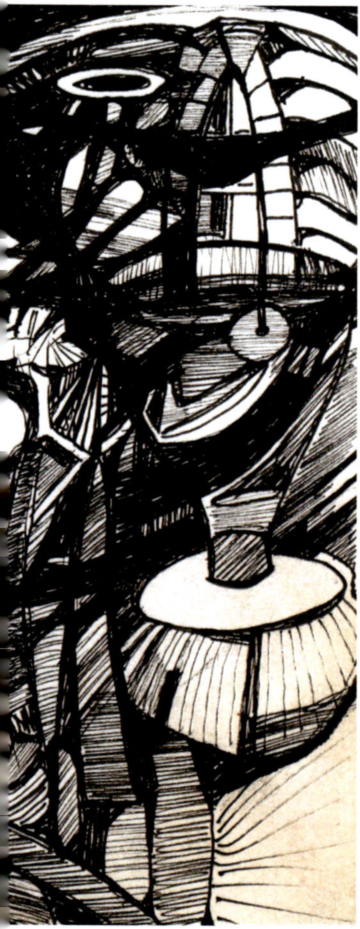

The Shout

The poetry of dreary weather

Marks on glass smeared together

Fingers touched the twixt between

Warm in cold out

Cold in warm out

A cloud of breath held the shout

Still for a moment in clag in clay

A red nose froze a man

Then gone still

Cacophony of grey

And brown and town

Silted poetry dredged and drudged

Marks on paper smudged together

His noise

Reflects the shine

On well versed leather.

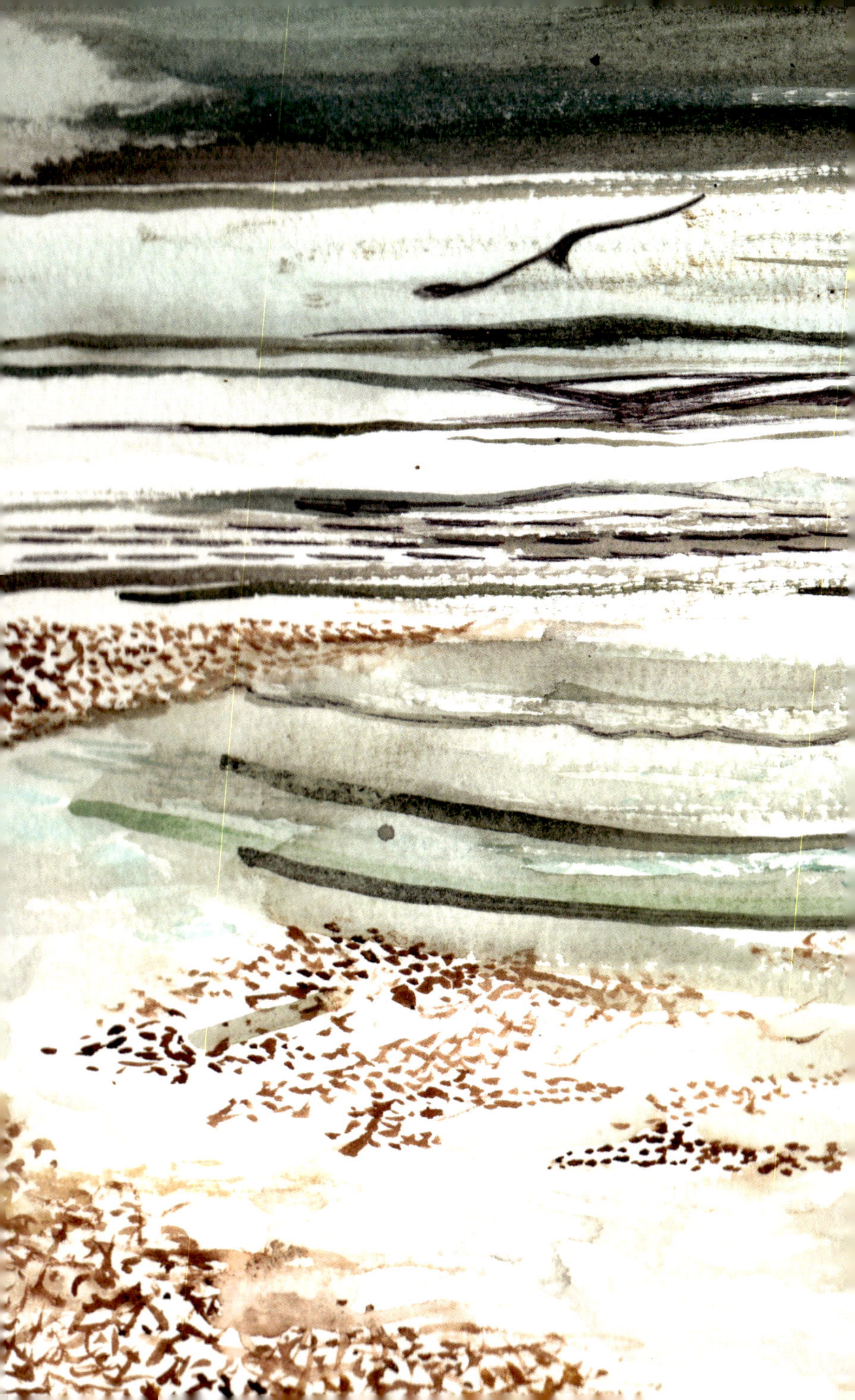

Doggerland

The old land fractured
Distal and potlid
Flint upon flint
A flick of an eyelid
The old man subsided
Atlantis divided
And the waves
Broke the skeleton
In proximal dark water
Let Doggerland go
Sand to ash coloured hand
North Sea let loose
The archipeligos's
Radial hand.

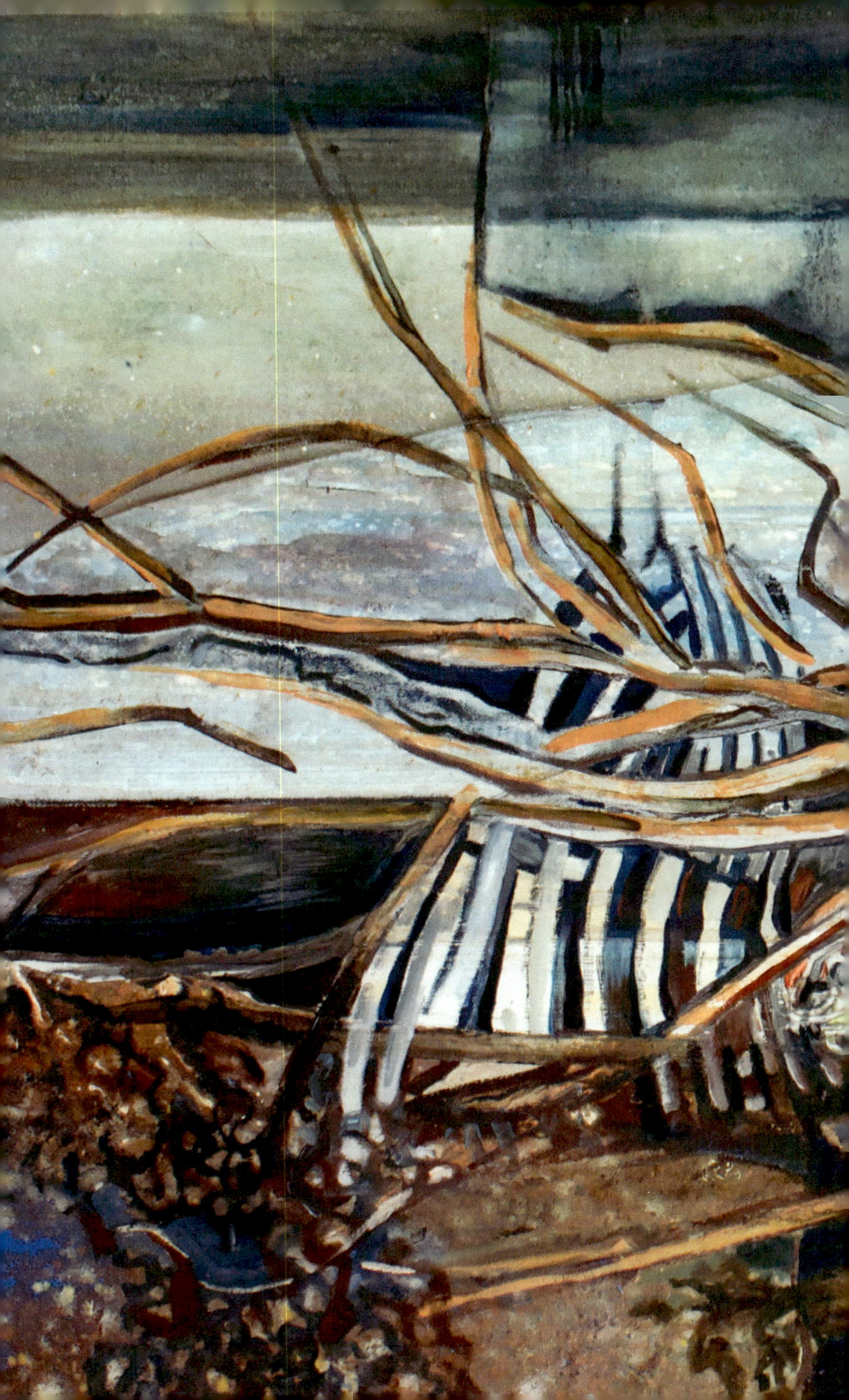

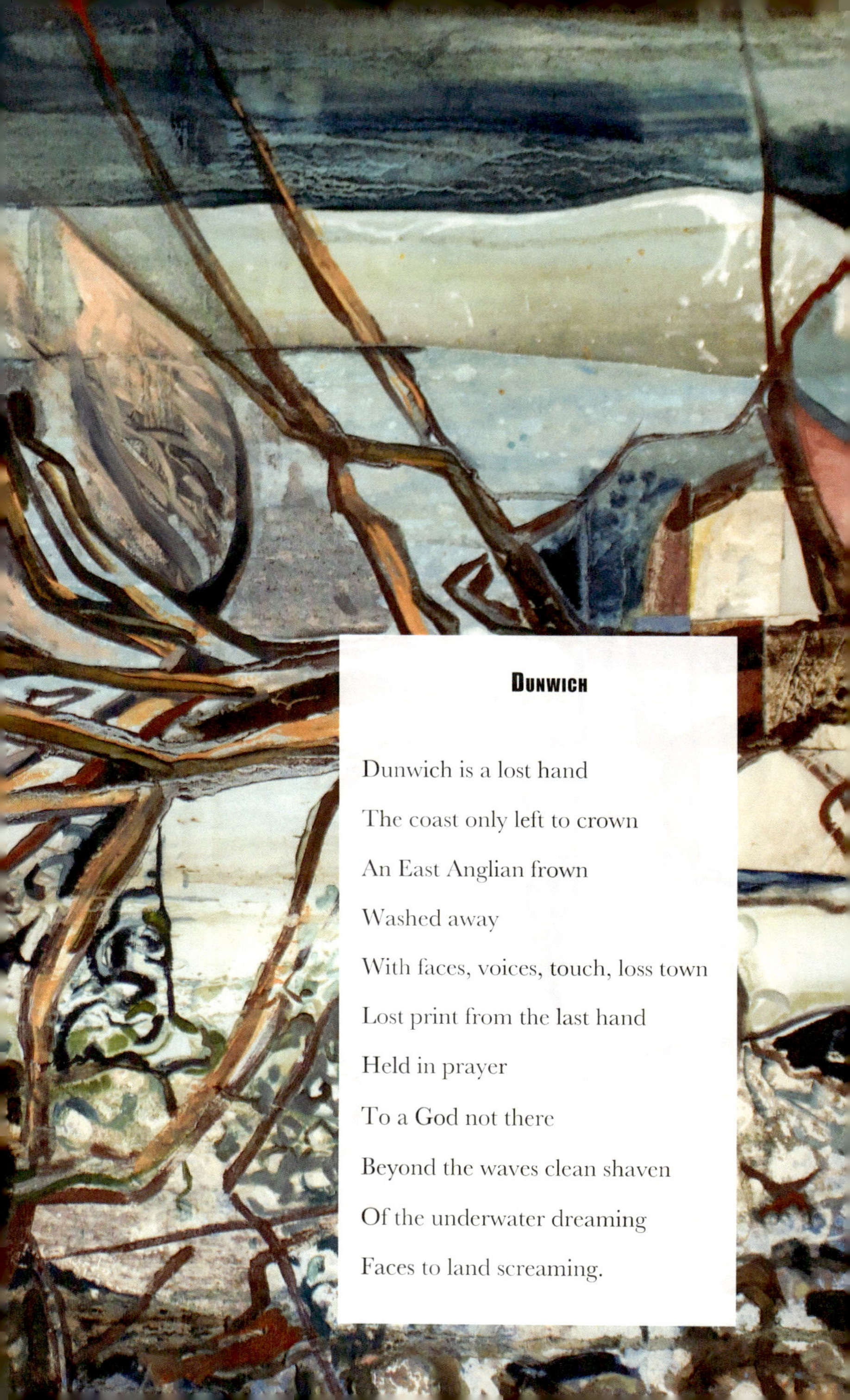

Dunwich

Dunwich is a lost hand
The coast only left to crown
An East Anglian frown
Washed away
With faces, voices, touch, loss town
Lost print from the last hand
Held in prayer
To a God not there
Beyond the waves clean shaven
Of the underwater dreaming
Faces to land screaming.

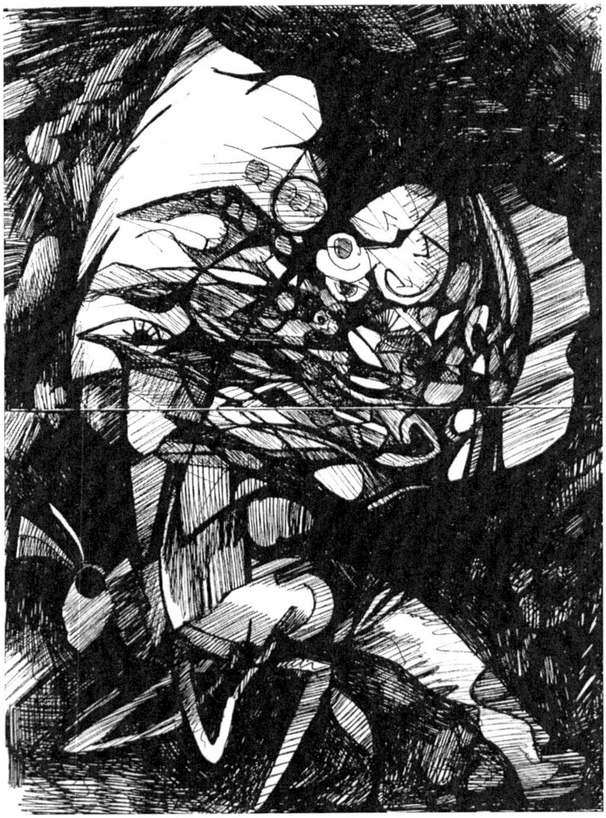

The Apology

I took a call on the dog and bone

The apology like histology was benign

And urgent like a cut

To find the merit

Of the cancerous angelic.

The hands on the clock face

Were stopped and made of lace

For the sorry to drip through

And we knew that time was lent

To wring out any good

On his forehead

The sticks and stones had broken

For words and crumbs effect.

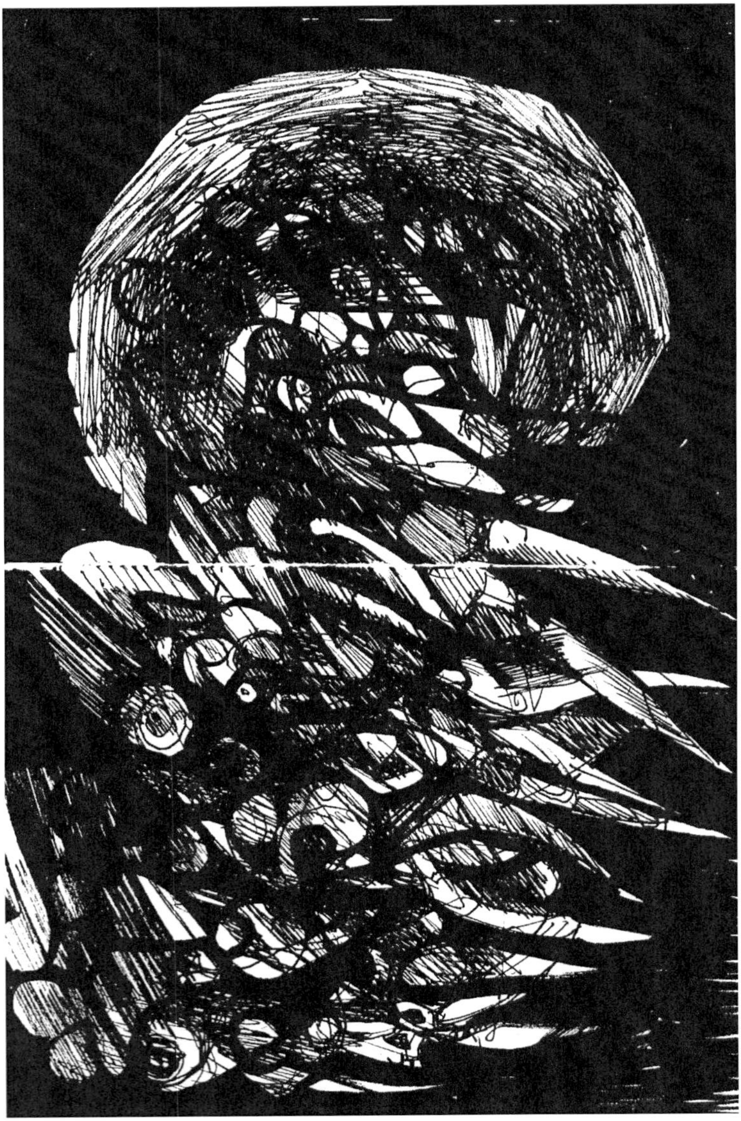

Never There

The shadows of another day
The mists that make hay
Or vice versa
Sunlight banishing night
And turning round
To grip a sound
That simply isn't there.
These are the soliloquies of maybe
Randomly day by day
Which we dream of everywhere.

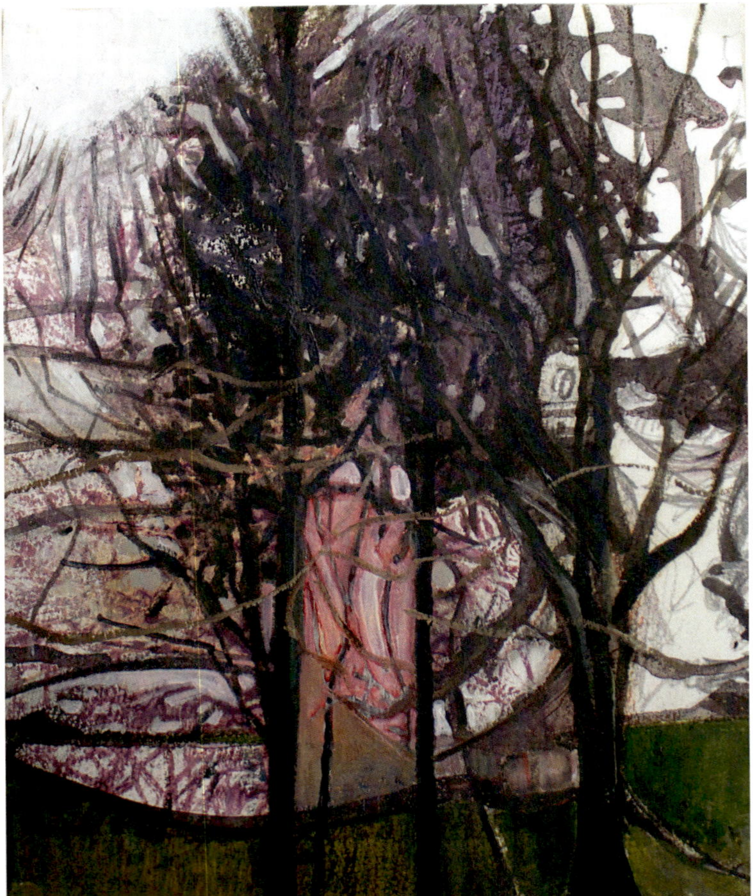

Shortest Day

Shortest day is as long as any other
How many Ursids
Will I see?
Shaken from a tail
Or a comet no matter
As I glance at the North Star
I'm as any other
Plotting a route
Across tidal Earth
In the ink stained difference
Between now and another.

Illustrations by the Author

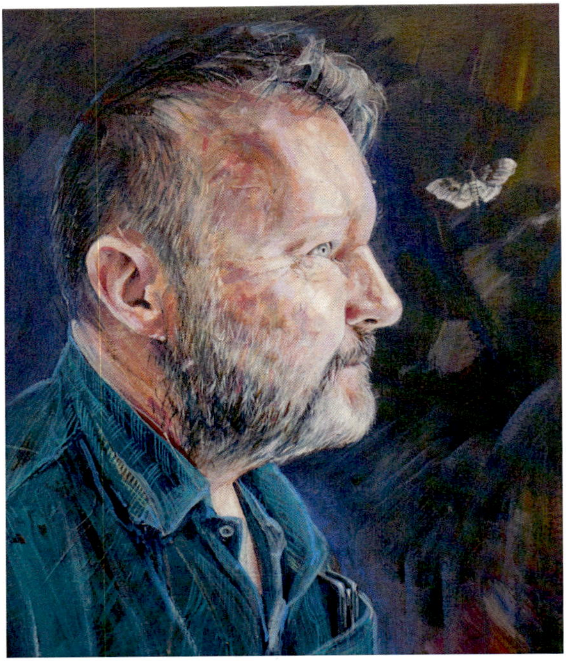

Portrait of Stephen Kirin
Acrylic on board by Lorna Kirin

About the Author

Stephen Kirin writes poetry and makes art in rural West Suffolk. He was born in Cambridge in 1966 and apart from a few years in London and a couple of years in Greece, has lived in East Anglia all his life. He is married for the second time to his wife and artistic collaborator Lorna and has 2 children and 2 step children.

His inspiration comes from the environment and the fascinating history around him, particularly in 2 acres of ancient woodland nearby, which he manages to a permaculture model. Also, in no small way, he follows in his father's footsteps, who wrote poetry all his life.

Most days are spent translating the life around him into messages that can be carried. This small volume is about these messages.

His poetry and short fiction have been frequently published in several anthologies.

For further information, please visit www.stephenkirin.com

and for his collaborations with Lorna; www.thekirins.com